ASIAPAC COMIC SERIES

The Silence of
the Wise

The Sayings of Lao Zi Book 2

Edited & illustrated by
Tsai Chih Chung

Translated by
Koh Kok Kiang

ASIAPAC . SINGAPORE

Publisher
ASIAPAC BOOKS PTE LTD
629 Aljunied Road
#04-06 Cititech Industrial Building
Singapore 1438
Tel: 7453868
Fax: 7453822
(as from 1 January 1993)

First published May 1992
Reprinted June 1993

ISBN 9971-985-89-6

Cover Design by Bay Song Lin
Typeset by Quaser Technology Pte Ltd
Printed in Singapore by Loi Printing Pte Ltd

Publisher' Note

After obtaining a good introduction to the teachings of Lao Zi, the founder of Taoism, from *The Sayings of Lao Zi,* it is time to take a step further by reading *The Sayings of Lao Zi Book 2*.

In it, Tsai Chih Chung has illustrated the more profound passages in the *Dao De Jing*, which have been excluded from his first book.

We feel honoured to be granted by well-known Taiwanese cartoonist Tsai Chih Chung the translation right to his bestselling comics. We would like also to take this opportunity to thank the translator and the typesetter for putting in their best effort in the production of this series.

Asiapac's new corporate identity design

The Asiapac Books corporate symbol has its original inspiration from the Chinese character for Asia. The central globe symbolizes the international market for which we publish and distribute books, thereby helping to bridge the East and the West. The open book resembling soaring wings represents Asiapac, ever dynamic and innovative, aiming to communicate with modern society through the printed page. The green colour expresses Asiapac's commitment to go "green for life".

About the Editor/Illustrator

Tsai Chih Chung was born in 1948 in Chang Hwa County of Taiwan. He began drawing cartoon strips at the age of 17. He worked as Art Director for Kuang Chi Programme Service in 1971. He founded the Far East Animation Production Company and the Dragon Cartoon Production Company in 1976, where he produced two cartoon films entitled *Old Master Q* and *Shao Lin Temple.*

Tsai Chih Chung first got his four-box comics published in newspapers and magazines in 1983. His funny comic characters such as the Drunken Swordsman, Fat Dragon, One-eyed Marshal and Bold Supersleuth have been serialized in the newspapers in Singapore, Malaysia, Taiwan, Hong Kong, Japan, Europe and the United States.

He was voted one of the Ten Outstanding Young People of Taiwan in 1985 and was acclaimed by the media and the academic circle in Taiwan.

The comic book *The Sayings of Zhuang Zi* was published in 1986 and marked a milestone in Tsai's career. Within two years, *Zhuang Zi* went into more than 70 reprints in Taiwan and 15 in Hong Kong and has to-date sold over one million copies.

In 1987, Tsai Chih Chung published *The Sayings of Lao Zi, The Sayings of Confucius* and two book based on Zen. Since then, he has published more than 20 titles, out of which 10 are about ancient Chinese thinkers and the rest based on historical and literary classics. All these books topped the bestsellers' list at one time or another. They have been translated into other languages such as Japanese, Korean, Thai. Asiapac is the publisher for the English version of these comics.

Tsai Chih Chung can be said to be the pioneer in the art of visualizing Chinese literature and philosophy by way of comics.

Introduction

The Dao De Jing (Classic of the Tao and its power of Goodness) is the most widely translated of all Chinese philosophical classics; there are more than 40 translations in the English language alone.

It contains slightly more than 5,000 Chinese characters and is divided into two books. This is probably done simply to confirm the statement in the biography of Lao Zi by Han dynasty historian Sima Qian that he wrote a work in two books at the request of the Keeper of the Pass.

There is some controversy in scholarly circles over whether Lao Zi as a historical figure ever existed, but there is no doubt about the intrinsic truth expressed in the Dao De Jing.

At the time the Dao De Jing was written, the author could not find any suitable description of the "sacred something" that was eternal and beyond life and death. Therefore he said:

> "Something there is,
> Before Heaven and Earth existed,
> Silent and void,
> Standing alone and changing not,
> Eternally it goes on and on.
> It is worthy to be the Mother of All Things.
> I do not know its name, so I called it the Tao."

The author was also aware of the limitations of thought and the human tendency to conceptualize things . Therefore he sounded a cautionary note in the very first passage of the Dao De Jing:

> " The Tao that can be spoken of not the Eternal Tao.
> The names that can be given are not absolute names."

Most scholars agree that the Dao De Jing as we know it today is the work of more than one author or compiler. The book often reads like an anthology of Taoist writings. We shall never know what Lao Zi originally wrote, if indeed there was such a work.

Many chapters fall into sections that sometimes appear to have connection with one another.

Perhaps for this reason, Tsai Chih Chung has not followed the traditional sequence in his rendering of the Dao De Jing in cartoon form. He has arranged the passages according to what he feels would make smooth reading for his readers.

In Tsai Chih Chung's hands, the timeless appeal of the Dao De Jing comes alive for the first time in the form of cartoons.

Koh Kok Kiang

About the Translator

Koh Kok Kiang is a journalist by vocation and a quietist by inclination. His interest in cultural topics and things of the mind started in his schooling years. It is his wish to discover the wisdom of the East that has kindled his interest in the Eastern philosophy. He has also translated other titles in Asiapac Comic Series, namely, *Book of Zen, Origins of Zen, Sayings of Lie Zi* and Book 1 of *Sayings of Lao Zi.*

Contents

The Sayings of Lao Zi
Book 2

Lao Zi

The legend of Lao Zi was recorded by the Han Dynasty historian Sima Qian as follows:

Lao Zi's family name was Li and his given name was Er. He was styled Tan. He came from the Goodwill Corners section of Grindstone Village of Ku district in the state of Chu. He was a keeper of the imperial archives of the Zhou Dynasty. Lao Zi practised the Dao* (Way) and the De (Power of Goodness). He learned to do his work in self-effacement and anonymity.

For a long time he lived in Zhou, and when he saw that it was breaking up he left. At the frontier, the keeper of the pass Yin Xi said, "Since you are going into seclusion, sir, I implore you to write me a book." So Lao Zi wrote a book in two parts, explaining Dao and De in something over five thousand characters. Then he went away. No one knew what became of him and where he died.

*Dao is the correct Hanyu Pinyin of Tao. This edition will use Tao, the more familiar form.

Life is eternal

1
The Tao is eternal. It is the source of heaven and earth and all things. It is the mysterious creative force.
2
This creative force is the essence of life.
道
3
It does not have any fixed form yet it exists always.
4
Its usefulness is unlimited and inexhaustible.

The mystery of Tao

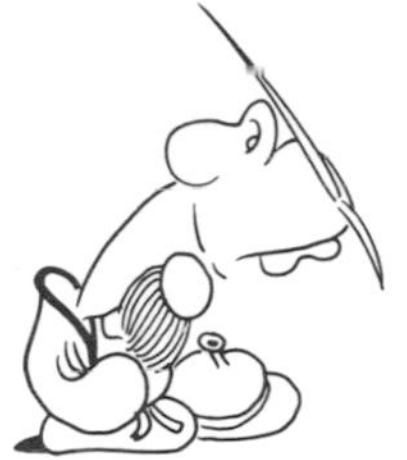

That which cannot be seen is formless.

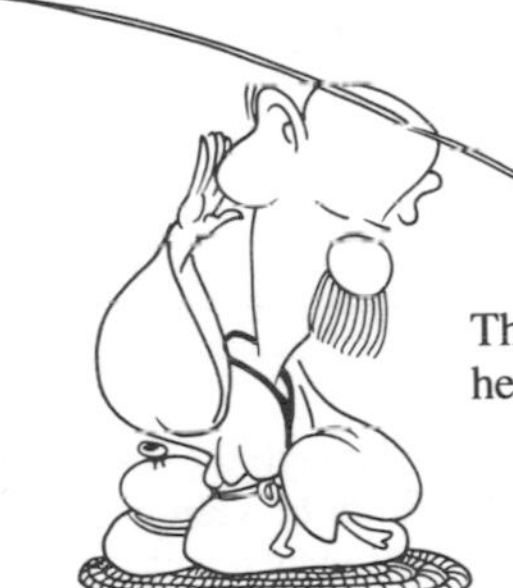

That which cannot be heard is noiseless.

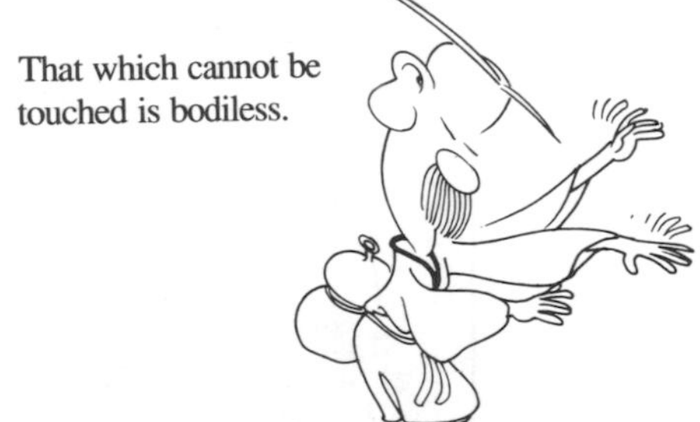

That which cannot be touched is bodiless.

The Tao has no colour, sound or shape and cannot be examined bit by bit for it is really one indivisible whole.

When it comes and goes, there is no light or darkness. Unceasing and eternal, it cannot be defined. It is always changing and reverting to the state of nothingness. That is why it is called the Form of the Formless, the Image of Nothingness. Hence it is Elusive.
5
6
Facing it, one cannot see its head; pursuing it, one cannot see its tail.
Tao
Tao
7
Abide by the Tao of old even if you live in the now. This understanding of the primal beginnings is the clue to Tao.
Though the Tao cannot be seen, heard or touched, yet it is beyond time, space and manifestation. Though in itself it has no form, yet it is the origin of all things.

The man of Tao

1
The ancients who lived in accord with Tao were men of subtle wisdom and penetrating intelligence. They were so profound that others did not understand them.
2
Since they were not easily understood, we can only attempt a superficial description of them.
3
They were guarded in their movements. Like men crossing a frozen river in winter; how cautious!
4
They were retiring as though shy of people.
As if all around there were danger; how watchful!

Their demeanour was reverent as though they were meeting honoured guests.
As if there were guests on every occasion; how dignified!

5

They quickly adapted themselves to any circumstances.
Like the ice melting in spring; how self-effacing!

6

7

Their manners were simple and artless.
Like an unhewn wood; how genuine!

Their minds were expansive.
Like a hollow valley awaiting a visitor; how receptive!

8

9

Their views were impartial and tolerant.
Like an expanse of water that collects everything; looking so turbid!

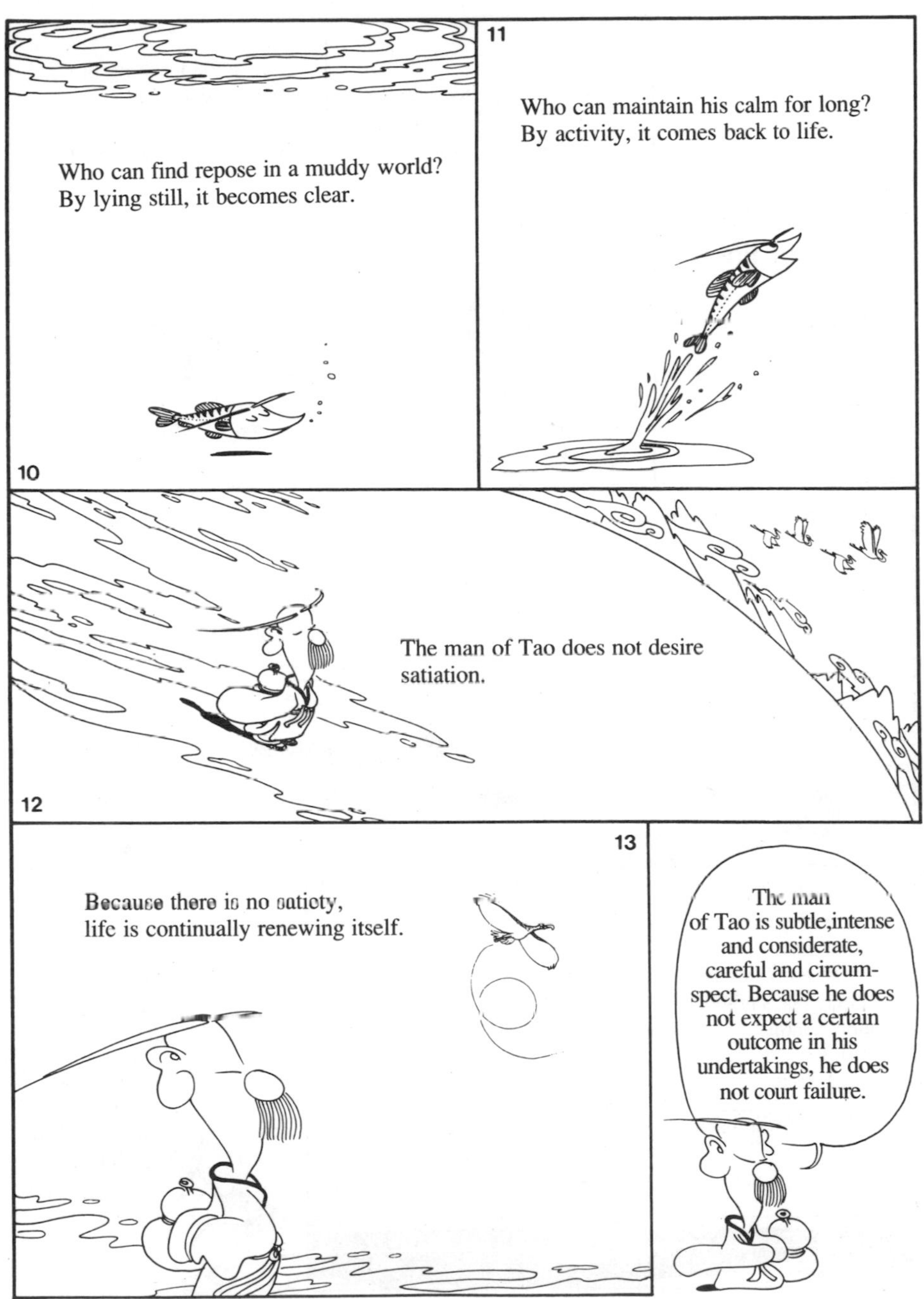

Who can find repose in a muddy world?
By lying still, it becomes clear.
10
11
Who can maintain his calm for long?
By activity, it comes back to life.
The man of Tao does not desire satiation.
12
13
Because there is no satiety,
life is continually renewing itself.
The man of Tao is subtle,intense and considerate, careful and circumspect. Because he does not expect a certain outcome in his undertakings, he does not court failure.

Simplicity of life

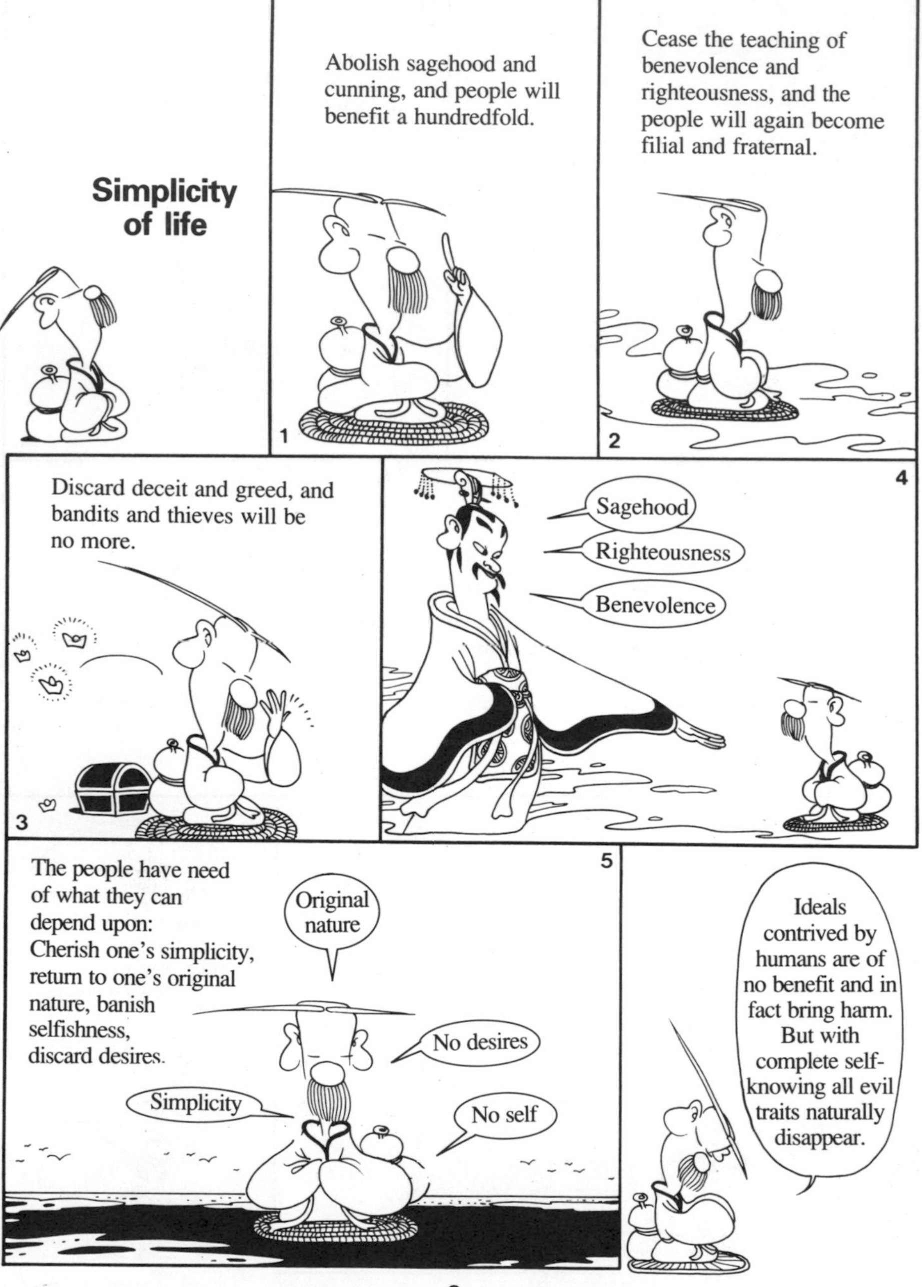

Tao as the essence
The conduct of the man of goodness is always in accord with the Tao.
道
1
Tao
Though the Tao seems insubstantial, within it there is substance.
2
Though the Tao seems intangible, within it there is form.
Tao
3
Tao
Though it seems vague and insubstantial, yet it includes everything in the universe and is the origin of all things.
4

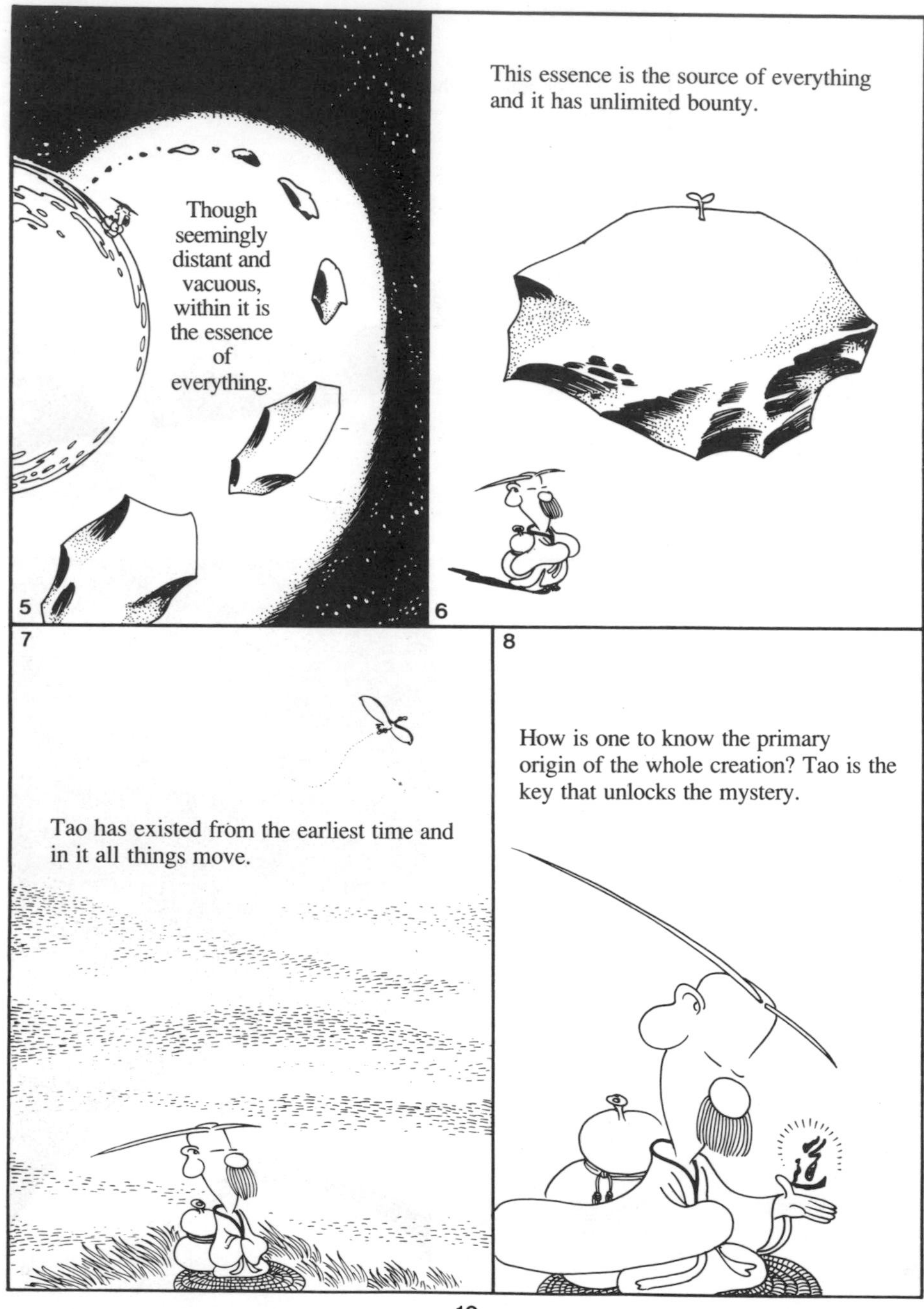
5
Though seemingly distant and vacuous, within it is the essence of everything.
This essence is the source of everything and it has unlimited bounty.
6
7
Tao has existed from the earliest time and in it all things move.
8
How is one to know the primary origin of the whole creation? Tao is the key that unlocks the mystery.
道

Oneness with the Tao

Everything that one does must happen naturally.

1

2

For that reason a storm does not last the whole morning.

And a downpour does not last the whole day.

3

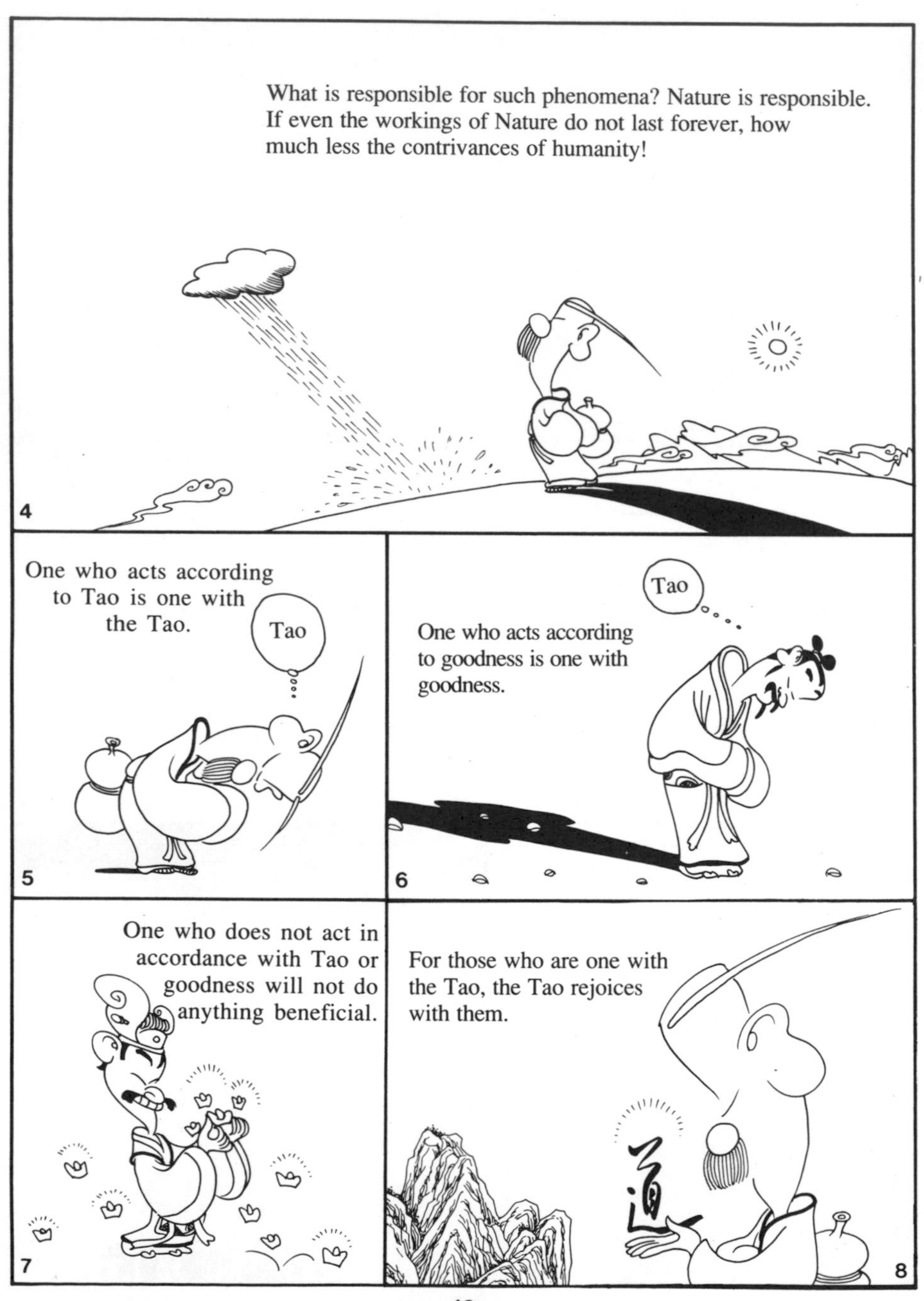
What is responsible for such phenomena? Nature is responsible. If even the workings of Nature do not last forever, how much less the contrivances of humanity!
4
One who acts according to Tao is one with the Tao.
Tao
5
Tao
One who acts according to goodness is one with goodness.
6
One who does not act in accordance with Tao or goodness will not do anything beneficial.
7
For those who are one with the Tao, the Tao rejoices with them.
道
8

9

For those who are one with goodness, goodness also rejoices with them.

10

For those who believe only in self-gain, they will have to live with the consequences.

No class!

Lacking in dignity.

11

For one lacking in honesty, no one will trust or be sincere towards them.

In action, be natural. Act for the common good and not for self-gain. This is because even natural phenomena do not endure forever, much less the works of humanity!

Conceit

He who raises himself on tiptoe to feel taller cannot stand firm.
1
He who strains his strides cannot go far.
2
3
He who is complacent is not enlightened.
My essay is excellent!
Nothing special!
4
He who is conceited cannot tell right from wrong.
My analysis is accurate!
Wrong!
Wrong!

5
He who is self-important is not supreme.
See how illustrious I am?
Showing himself off!
6
He who is pompous cannot be whole.
7
To the man of Tao, such inflating of the ego can be likened to having too much food and clothing. They are more of a hindrance than a help.
Pomposity
Conceit
Self-centredness
Self-assertion
Most people think it is good to be famous and successful, but the man of Tao eschews this.
!
Let things happen naturally and do not try to force a certain outcome. That which is not natural will not be right.
8

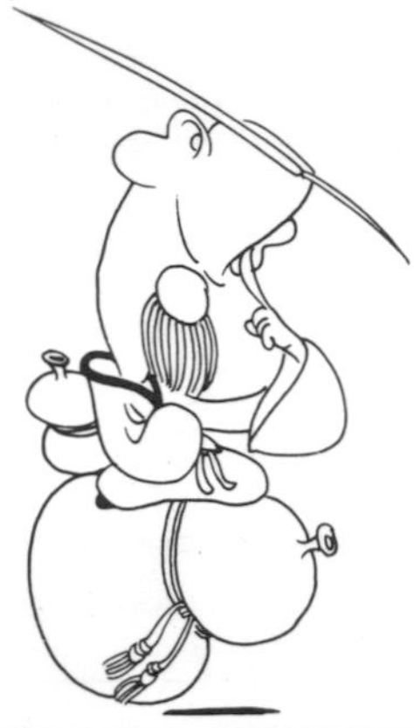

Origin of things

1

Something mysterious yet complete existed before heaven and earth.

2

Silent and alone, it is eternal and embraces all.

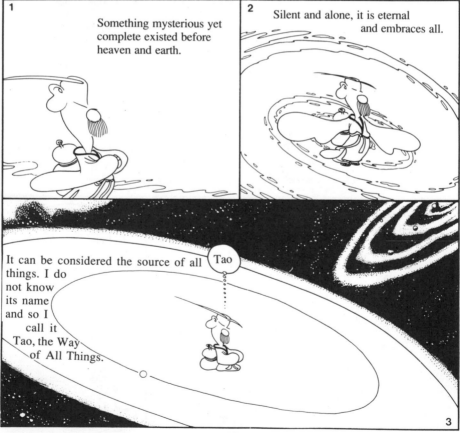

It can be considered the source of all things. I do not know its name and so I call it Tao, the Way of All Things.

Tao

3

If one has to describe it, one can say it is great. Being great implies reaching out in space. Reaching out in space implies far-reaching.
4

There is going and there is coming. Everything returns to nothingness.
5

6
Therefore it is said: Tao is great, Heaven is great, Earth is great, Humanity is great. Within the universe are all things and humans are one with thc universe.

7
Man is in harmony with Earth, Earth harmonises with Heaven, Heaven harmonises with Tao, and the Tao harmonises with what is natural.

Tao produces all things and they undergo constant change. Whatever is one with the Tao is eternal and has unlimited use. Tao has no motive for producing things and is merely abiding by its nature.

The right foundation

Though he may be surrounded by splendour and comfort, he is always reposeful and disinterested.

4

How then should a king conduct himself before all under heaven?

5

If one is flippant and takes things too lightly, he will easily lose what is fundamental. But if one is too eager to act, he will never know peace and quietude.

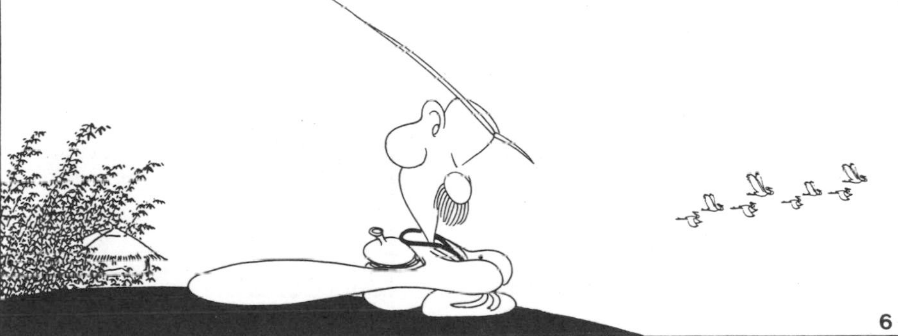

6

The heavy can resist the light, the light can go around the heavy. An administrator should observe the light when dealing with the heavy and know when to be flexible. If not, he will bring harm to himself and those around him.

Tao in action

1
Good conduct leaves behind no traces.
2
Good words afford no room for criticism.
3
Good mathematicians require no abacus.
4
Good doors need no bolts, and are not easily opened.

Good teachers do not need anything to bind their students to them.

5

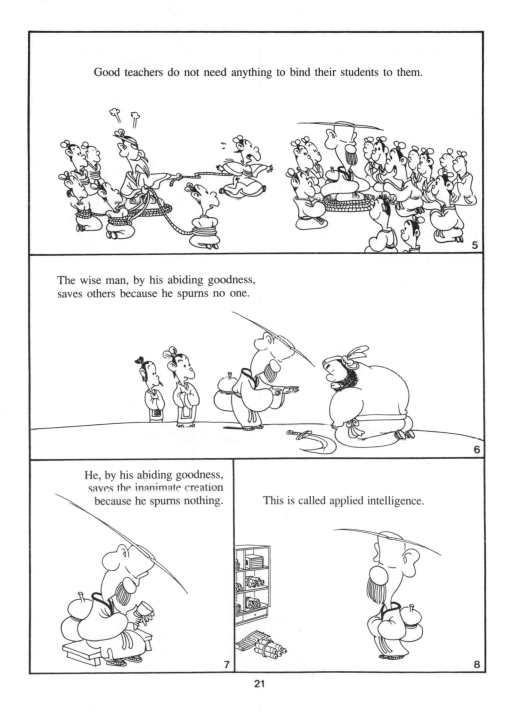

The wise man, by his abiding goodness, saves others because he spurns no one.

6

He, by his abiding goodness, saves the inanimate creation because he spurns nothing.

7

This is called applied intelligence.

8

Therefore the good man is the bad man's teacher.
You should learn from him!
9
And the bad man can serve as a lesson for the good man.
I must not be like him.
10
When one fails to esteem his teacher...
Why must I learn from him?
11
...Or the other fails to value his lesson,
Such a man is to be despised!
12
Each is under a great delusion, though each may be learned.
13
The sage follows his nature in his relationship with people and the world at large. He is able to treat the good and the bad with goodness for he has no ego.

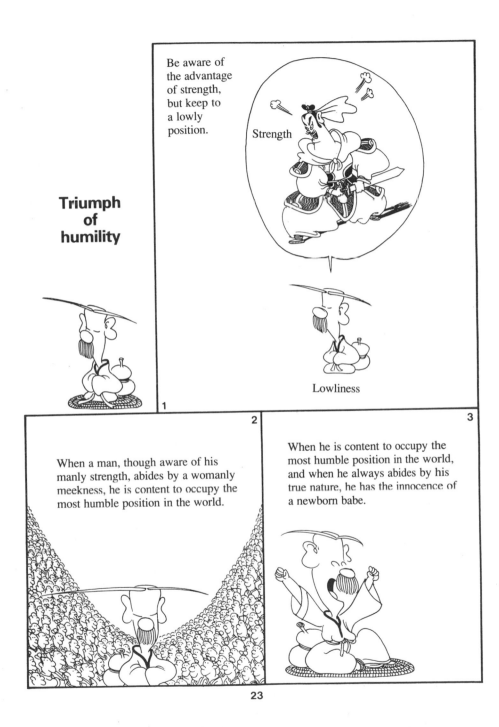

Triumph of humility

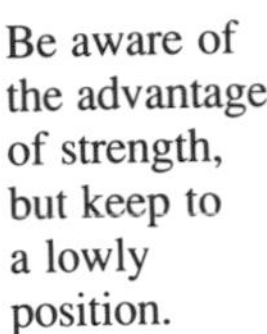

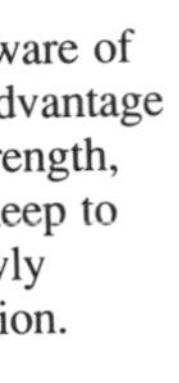

Be aware of the advantage of strength, but keep to a lowly position.

Lowliness

When a man, though aware of his manly strength, abides by a womanly meekness, he is content to occupy the most humble position in the world.

When he is content to occupy the most humble position in the world, and when he always abides by his true nature, he has the innocence of a newborn babe.

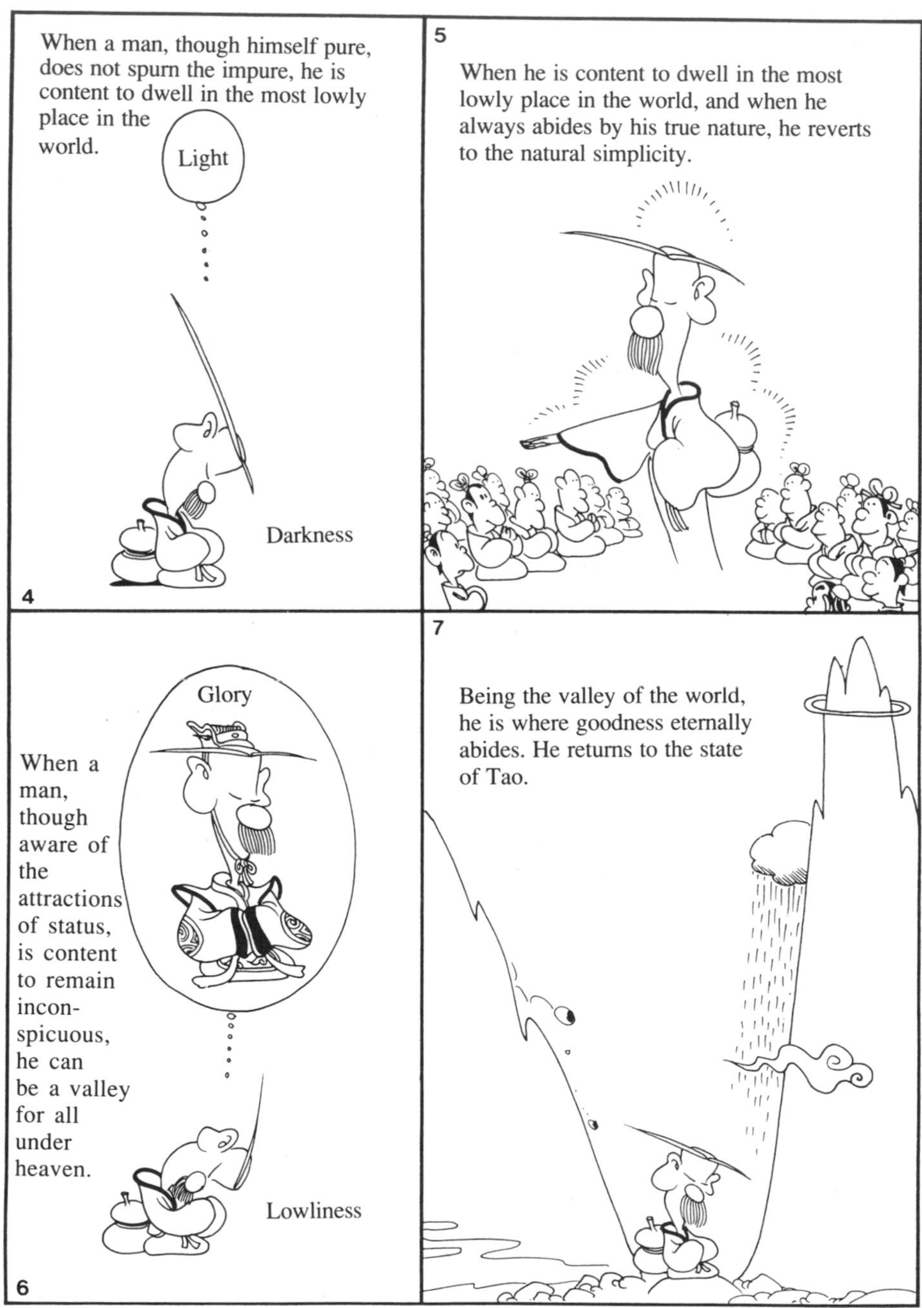
4
When a man, though himself pure, does not spurn the impure, he is content to dwell in the most lowly place in the world.
Light
Darkness
5
When he is content to dwell in the most lowly place in the world, and when he always abides by his true nature, he reverts to the natural simplicity.
6
When a man, though aware of the attractions of status, is content to remain incon-spicuous, he can be a valley for all under heaven.
Glory
Lowliness
7
Being the valley of the world, he is where goodness eternally abides. He returns to the state of Tao.

8
It is the Tao which brings all things into being.
9
When the sage abides by purity, he is a leader among men.
10
Hence if one wants to prevail in the world, one must let things happen naturally and not try to scheme to make things happen.
One has to preserve purity and harmony so that things occur spontaneously. Only in this way will one not cause contention in the world.

The futility of force
1
As for those who would take the world and forcefully tinker as they see fit, I observe that they never succeed.
2
For the world is a sacred vessel not made to be altered by man. The tinkerer who applies force will spoil things.
3
The usurper will lose everything.

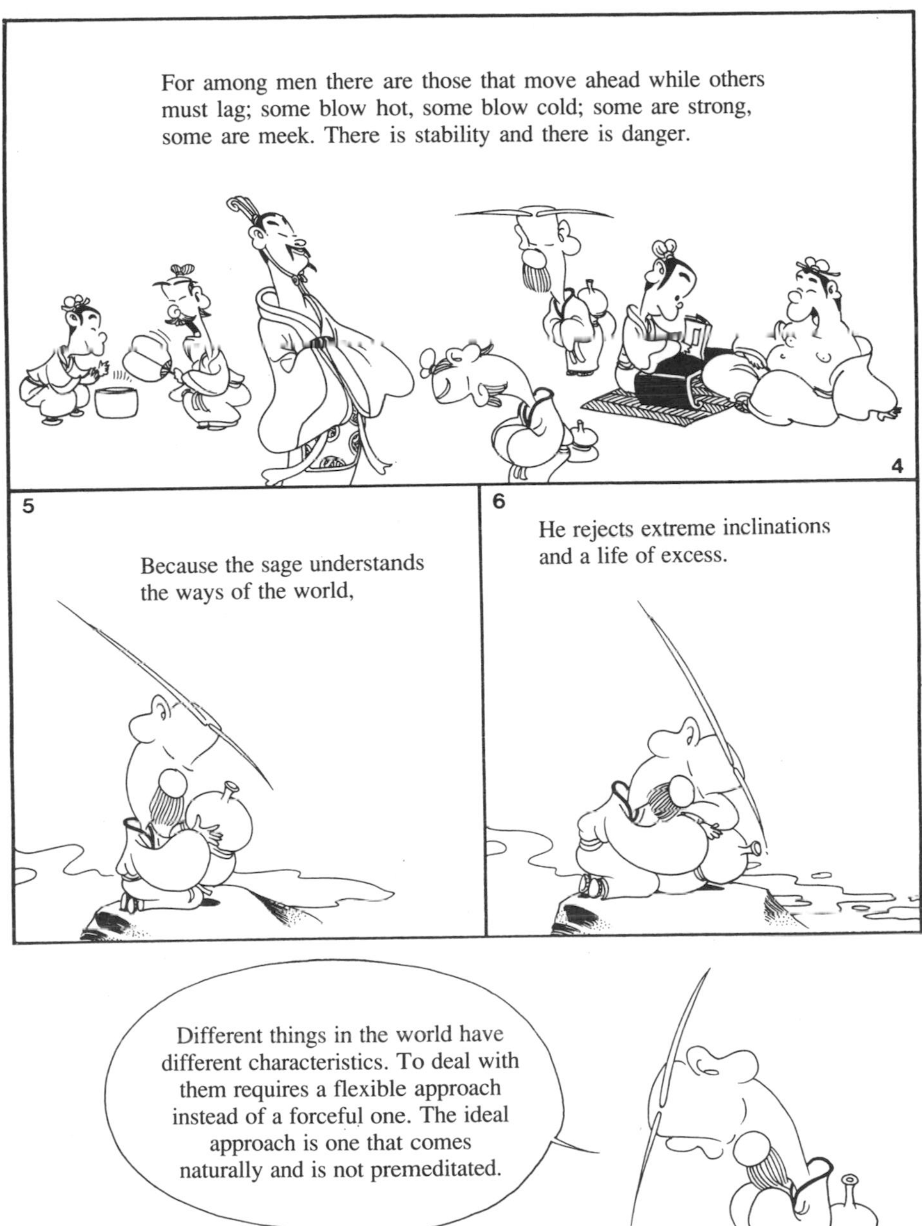
For among men there are those that move ahead while others must lag; some blow hot, some blow cold; some are strong, some are meek. There is stability and there is danger.
4
5
Because the sage understands the ways of the world,
6
He rejects extreme inclinations and a life of excess.
Different things in the world have different characteristics. To deal with them requires a flexible approach instead of a forceful one. The ideal approach is one that comes naturally and is not premeditated.

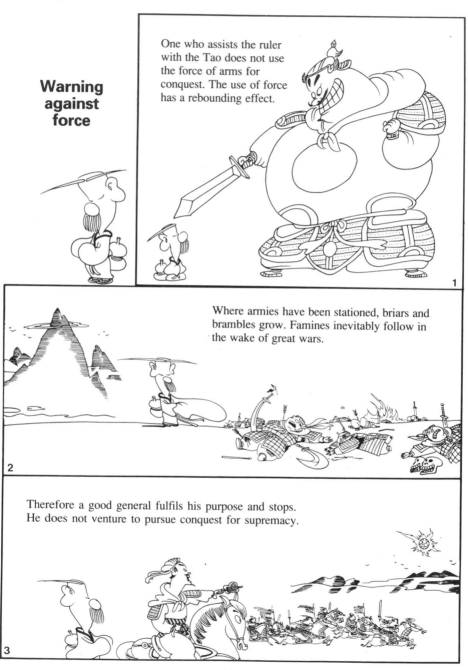

Warning against force

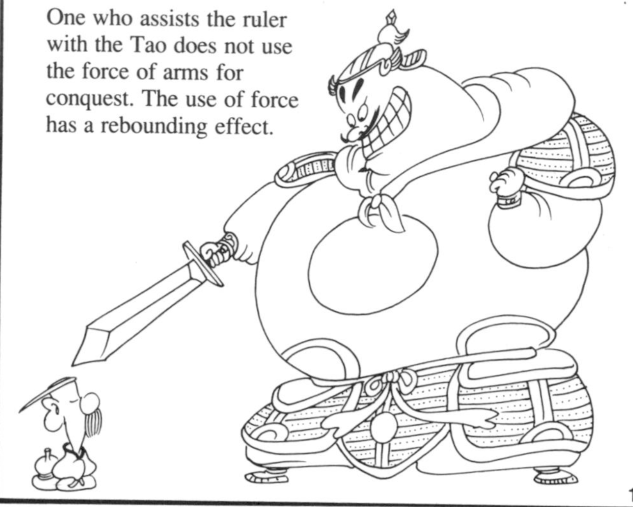

One who assists the ruler with the Tao does not use the force of arms for conquest. The use of force has a rebounding effect.
1

Where armies have been stationed, briars and brambles grow. Famines inevitably follow in the wake of great wars.

2

Therefore a good general fulfils his purpose and stops. He does not venture to pursue conquest for supremacy.

3

4

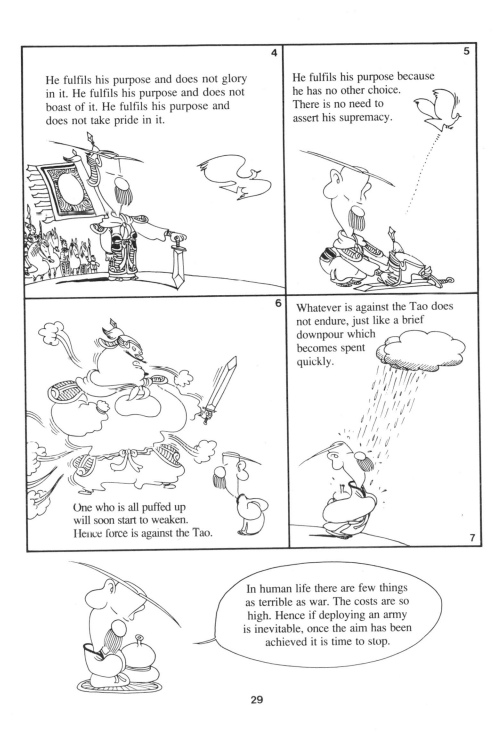

He fulfils his purpose and does not glory in it. He fulfils his purpose and does not boast of it. He fulfils his purpose and does not take pride in it.

5

He fulfils his purpose because he has no other choice. There is no need to assert his supremacy.

6

One who is all puffed up will soon start to weaken. Hence force is against the Tao.

Whatever is against the Tao does not endure, just like a brief downpour which becomes spent quickly.

7

In human life there are few things as terrible as war. The costs are so high. Hence if deploying an army is inevitable, once the aim has been achieved it is time to stop.

The function of Tao

1
Tao is absolute and eternally nameless. Though indistinct, the whole world cannot subjugate it.
2
If rulers can preserve the unspoiled nature of the Tao, all the people of the world shall yield them lordship of their own accord.
道
3
Because heaven and earth are one with Tao,
4
They produce rain and dew which benefit all humans alike without their asking.

Tao is responsible for creation and as soon as one begins to divide things up, there are names.

Purpose

Wealth

Name

5

Once there are names, one should also know when to stop. Knowing when to stop, one thereby avoids peril.

Fight for gain.

Fight for name.

6

7

Tao

Tao is to all creation as rivers are to seas.

All things come naturally from Tao and Tao nourishes all. If a ruler can act naturally and not according to whims and fancies, his subjects will submit themselves willingly.

Tao and creation

1
The Tao flows everywhere, it may go left or right. All things derive their life from it, yet it does not claim lordship over them.
It nourishes all things yet does not claim them as its own. Thus it can be called hidden and unseen.
2
It is the ultimate destiny of all animate creation though it is not conscious of it, and it may be considered great.
3
Because it is never conscious of its greatness,
4
It can achieve greatness.
5
The Tao produces and nourishes all things but does not claim lordship over them. This nature of the Tao serves as a useful lesson for rulers.

Tao acts silently

The Tao always abides by what is natural. It does not deliberately set out to do things, yet nothing is left undone.

1

If rulers abide by the Tao, the myriad creatures will of their own accord come under their influence.

2

3

When they of their own accord come under my influence and if selfish desires arise, I will restrain them with the nameless pristine simplicity.

Once restrained by the nameless simplicity, they will again be free from selfish desires. Thus free from selfish desires, they will be pure, and the world will of its own accord be peaceful.

4

Rulers ought to let people change by themselves. By not interfering with their inner development, they can avoid problems of discontent.

The fullness of Tao

Since antiquity,
whatever was one
with Tao was thus:
Heaven was one with Tao
and so the skies were clear.
1
2
Earth was one with Tao and so it was tranquil.
3
The spirits were one with Tao
and so they were divine.
4
The valleys were one with Tao
and so they were full.

The animate creation was one with Tao and so all things lived and grew.
5
It follows that: Without that which renders it clear, heaven is in danger of disruption.
6
The rulers were one with Tao, and so everything under heaven was put right. All these are the result of oneness with Tao.
7
8
Without that which renders it tranquil, Earth is in danger of being jolted.
9
Without that which renders them divine, the spirits are in danger of dissipation.

10
Without that which renders them full, the valleys are likely to dry up.
11
Without the life-giving power, all things will perish.
12
Without the Tao's uplifting power, the rulers are in danger of being overthrown.
13
The valuable and the valueless come from the same source.
Precious
Base
14
The high and low share the same foundation.
High
Low

The nobility depend on the common people for support. Therefore they call themselves "the orphaned", "the destitute" and "the unworthy". Isn't this proof that the common people are the base on which the highest rest?

15

Therefore the best kind of praise is no praise, because where there is expectation of praise, there is also fear of blame.

16

Don't be like the sparkling gem which becomes the object of human desire.

17

Rather be like the plain rock which people take no notice of.

18

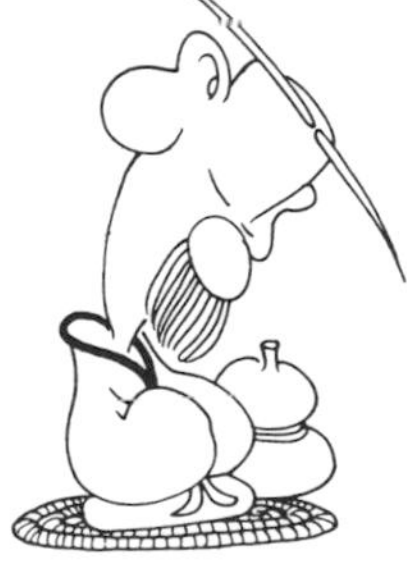

Because of Tao, there is the oneness of things. Everything rests on the Tao. Anything, however high, rests on something. Because without the base, nothing can have a place to stand.

Tao and human being

Tao
When the highest type of men hear of the Tao, they earnestly live in accordance with it.
Tao
1
When the average type of men hear of the Tao, they seem to be aware and yet unaware of it.
Tao
2
Tao
When the lowest type of men hear of the Tao, they laugh at it loudly.
3
If they did not laugh at it, it would not be the Tao.
If a person of your calibre can understand the Tao, then it would not be the Tao.
4
Hence in antiquity there was this saying:
5

The one who understands the Tao may outwardly appear dull of comprehension:
He doesn't look impressive.
Yes.
6
He who is advanced in Tao seems to slip backwards.
7
The straight and direct Tao seems to be bumpy.
8
The man of highest integrity appears to be like a yawning chasm.
9
The most pure appears as though it were impure.
10
Ample integrity appears insufficient.
11

Dynamic integrity
appears apathetic.
12
13
Robust integrity appears
lethargic.
14
The great square has no corners.
15
The great vessel has no shape.

The great sound is inaudible.

16

The great form is formless.

17

18

The great Tao cannot be seen and has no name.

19

Only Tao can begin and complete the growth of things.

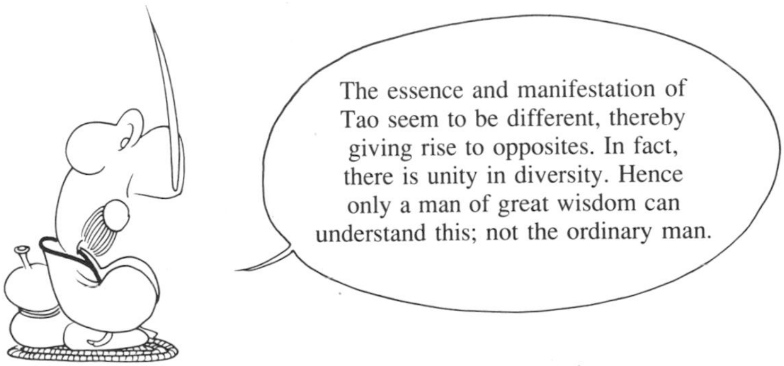

The essence and manifestation of Tao seem to be different, thereby giving rise to opposites. In fact, there is unity in diversity. Hence only a man of great wisdom can understand this; not the ordinary man.

Calm quietude

1

That which is most complete may seem to suffer insufficiency, but its usefulness is not thereby diminished.

2

That which is most abundant may seem empty, but its usefulness never fails.

3

The most straight may seem crooked.

The most skilful may seem clumsy.

4

The greatest eloquence may seem like stuttering.

5

6

Calm can overcome agitation, cold can overcome hot.

Calm

With a pure and silent mind, one can put things right everywhere under heaven.

7

The man of complete purity does not concern himself with his outward appearance but instead cherish his inner state. The Tao does not proclaim itself but it has unlimited power to act. He who can do that can be an example to the world.

The mystical goodness
1
The Tao gives birth to things.
2
De (the power of goodness) nurtures and sustains them.
3
With matter they take shape and the circumstances of the world give them their function. Tao and De are the foundation of being.
4
That is why all things do honour to the Tao and exalt its goodness.
5
Respect for the Tao and esteem for its goodness is not sought but occurs naturally.

So when the Tao gives birth to things, its goodness fosters them: They grow, arc fed, strengthened and sheltered until they come to ripe maturity.

6

The Tao gives birth but does not possess, acts but does not claim credit, rears but docs not control.

7

This is mystical power of the Tao.

8

When the Tao gives birth to things, it is but acting in accordance with its nature. It does not hold sway over things but allows things to grow naturally. It has no self-interest and therein lies its greatness. No wonder the Tao is esteemed!

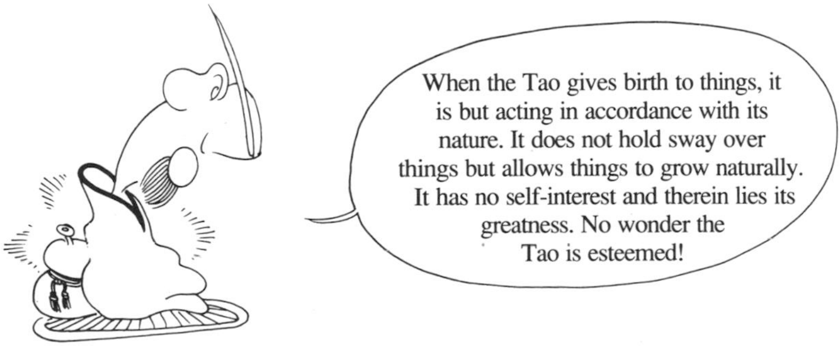

Let us call it Tao

1
Everything under heaven has a beginning which may be thought of as the origin of things.
道
2
Calm
If we know the origin, we can say there is a mother of all under heaven and everything is its offspring.
3
If from the offspring one can perceive the Tao of the mother, then one's whole life may be preserved from harm.
4
Block off all the channels of desires. Close the gate of pleasure-seeking so that desire does not arise and one's whole life will be without exhaustion.
Ear
Will
Body
Eye
Nose
Tongue

5
Open the gate of pleasure-seeking and be busy fulfilling one's desires and one's whole life will be beyond salvation.
6
Seeing what is small is called insight.
7
Abiding in gentleness is called strength.
8
Use your light to return to insight.
9
Thus do not cause yourself distress. This is to abide in the Absolute (Tao).
By observing with a quiet and still mind, one can perceive the origin of things. This calm insight into the origin of desire ends desire naturally. When there is no centre to give rise to desire, one sees things as they originally are.

The right teaching
1
If I have even a bit of intelligence, I will take the way of the great Tao and exercise care...
2
...Lest I deviate from it to a narrow bypath.
3
The empty way of the great Tao is most easy to travel, yet people prefer the busy little bypaths.
4
Because of self-aggrandizement, the court is in turmoil,
Fight!
Speak!
5
The fields are overgrown with weeds,

8

They are sated with food and wine and have more possessions than they could ever use.

Such people are no better than the chief of bandits. Surely this is not the Way.

Those in a position of authority should act without self-interest and should not pursue their desires and seek self-gain. Otherwise they are no better than robbers.

One and the world

1
What is firmly established cannot be uprooted.
2
What is securely held cannot slip away.
德
3
When the Tao and goodness are established, they will continue and benefit not just oneself but also later generations.
4
When one's conduct is in accordance with Tao,
5
The inherent qualities become real.

When a whole family follows Tao, the inherent qualities become abundant. When a whole village follows Tao, the inherent qualities become enduring. When the whole state follows Tao, the inherent qualities become multiplied. When all under heaven follows Tao, the inherent qualities become universal.
6
Hence if I abide in goodness, and have no self-image, I can be like a mirror to others.
7
Observe other persons through your own person.
8
Observe other families through your own family. Observe other villages through your own village. Observe other states through your own state. Observe the past and future of everything under heaven through the present state of everything under heaven.
9
How do I know the nature of all heaven? Through this.
10
To cultivate oneself is like consolidating a foundation and it is the basic requirement for a right relationship with others. When one has goodness, one can then see what is wrong with others.

Qualities of a baby

1
He who has complete goodness has the innocence and guilelessness of a newborn babe.
Hee! Hee!
2
The infant has no knowledge of things and is weak and vulnerable, but still it acts with pure naturalness, and so the venomous insects do not sting or bite it.
3
The wild beasts will not attack him and birds of prey will not seize him.
4
His bones are soft and his sinews tender, yet his grip is firm.

5

Although he knows nothing about the sexual union between male and female, yet his organs are complete. This is because his vital force is intact.

He cries the whole day without becoming hoarse. This is because his person is a harmony.

Wah!

6

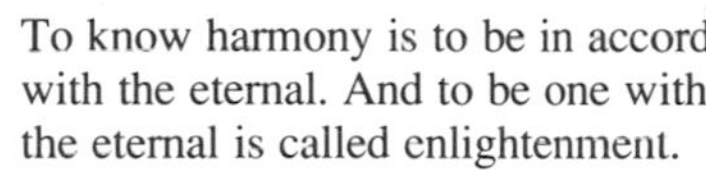

To know harmony is to be in accord with the eternal. And to be one with the eternal is called enlightenment.

7

8

If one is ignorant of the eternal and for selfish reasons uses ways and means then one will court disaster.

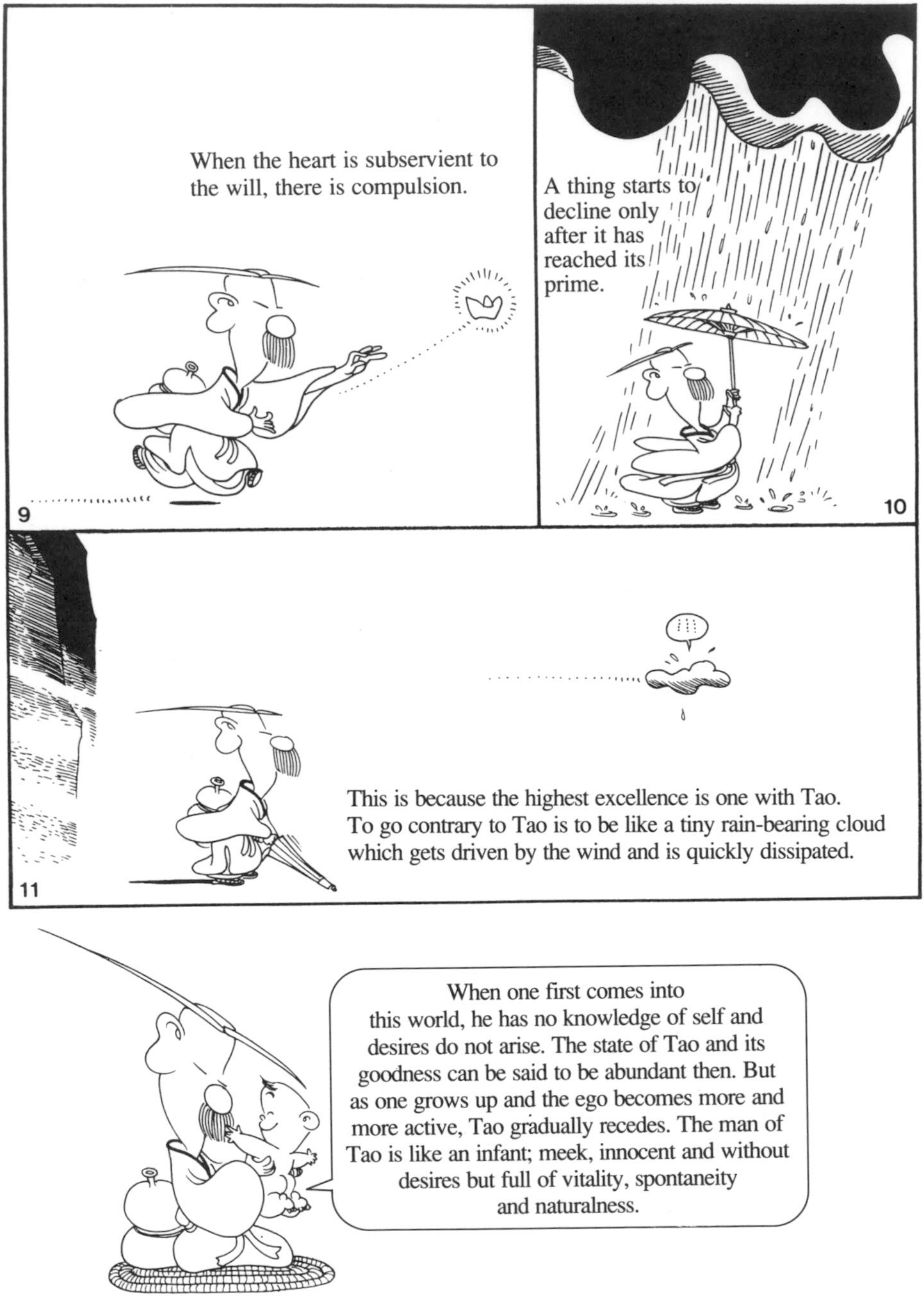

When the heart is subservient to the will, there is compulsion.

9

A thing starts to decline only after it has reached its prime.

10

This is because the highest excellence is one with Tao. To go contrary to Tao is to be like a tiny rain-bearing cloud which gets driven by the wind and is quickly dissipated.

11

When one first comes into this world, he has no knowledge of self and desires do not arise. The state of Tao and its goodness can be said to be abundant then. But as one grows up and the ego becomes more and more active, Tao gradually recedes. The man of Tao is like an infant; meek, innocent and without desires but full of vitality, spontaneity and naturalness.

Good and bad government

The right may turn out to be wrong.
The good may turn out to be evil.
Evil
Good
Indeed people do not realize the truth of this and have been under a delusion for such a long time.
The sage, though he is strict in his own conduct, does not require other men to conform.
Though he is sharp he does not malign others.
Though he is upright he is not high-handed.
Though he is bright, he does not dazzle other men.
Fortune or calamity, right or wrong, good or evil are not things that are fixed. Many people do not see both sides of a thing and hence in seeking gain they instead court disaster.

Embodiment of Tao

In governing people, the best way is to cherish purity of character.

Because one cherishes purity of character, he will follow the Tao before disaster befalls him.

To follow Tao means to adhere to its inherent qualities.

De

The inherent qualities of purity and naturalness allow one to have infinite capacity to do things.

5
He can overcome everything and no one knows the limits of his abilities.
6
If no one knows his limits, the administration of the state can be entrusted to him.
無為而治
7
When a person understands this principle, and is one with Tao, his state is eternal. This is called "sinking roots firm and deep, the way of eternal life and everlasting truth."
A life of simplicity enables one to cultivate one's inner life and to be in the state of complete purity.

Big and small countries

1
A big country should be like the delta where the streams descend. This is the concourse of the world.
2
The female, willing to occupy a lowly position, uses quietude to overcome the male.
3
Thus when a large nation shows deference to a small nation, it wins over the small nation. And when a small nation shows deference to a large nation, it is easily accepted by the large nation

4
One uses deference to make the small nation seek shelter in the large nation. The other uses deference to make the large nation magnanimous towards the small.
5
The large state wishes only to shelter and nurture the small state. The small state wishes only to join and work for the large state. Since both get what they want, it is fitting that the large state should be humble.
6
The small state shows deference and is able to preserve itself while the large state shows deference and gets others to become part of it.
The way for the large nations and small nations to co-exist is to show deference and not to be assertive. If they are in violent contention, the small nation will perish while the large nation will find that it cannot endure.

Tao as treasure

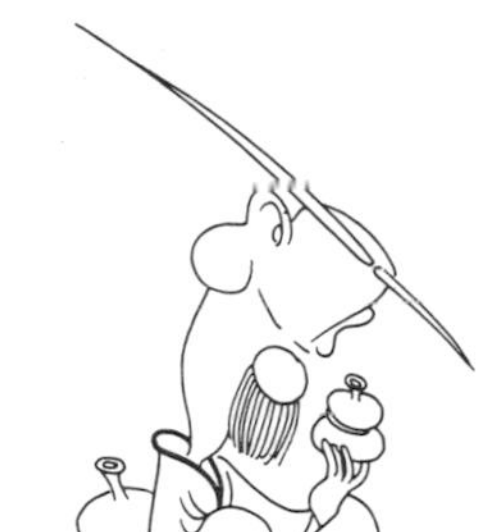

1

Tao is the most precious thing in the universe. The good man regards Tao as a treasure.

2

The bad man regards Tao as a refuge.

3

When a man of Tao speaks or acts, his words and actions are full of goodness and touch the heart. This earns him the respect of people. His existence can be a law of life to others. Hence bad people cannot afford to forsake the Tao.

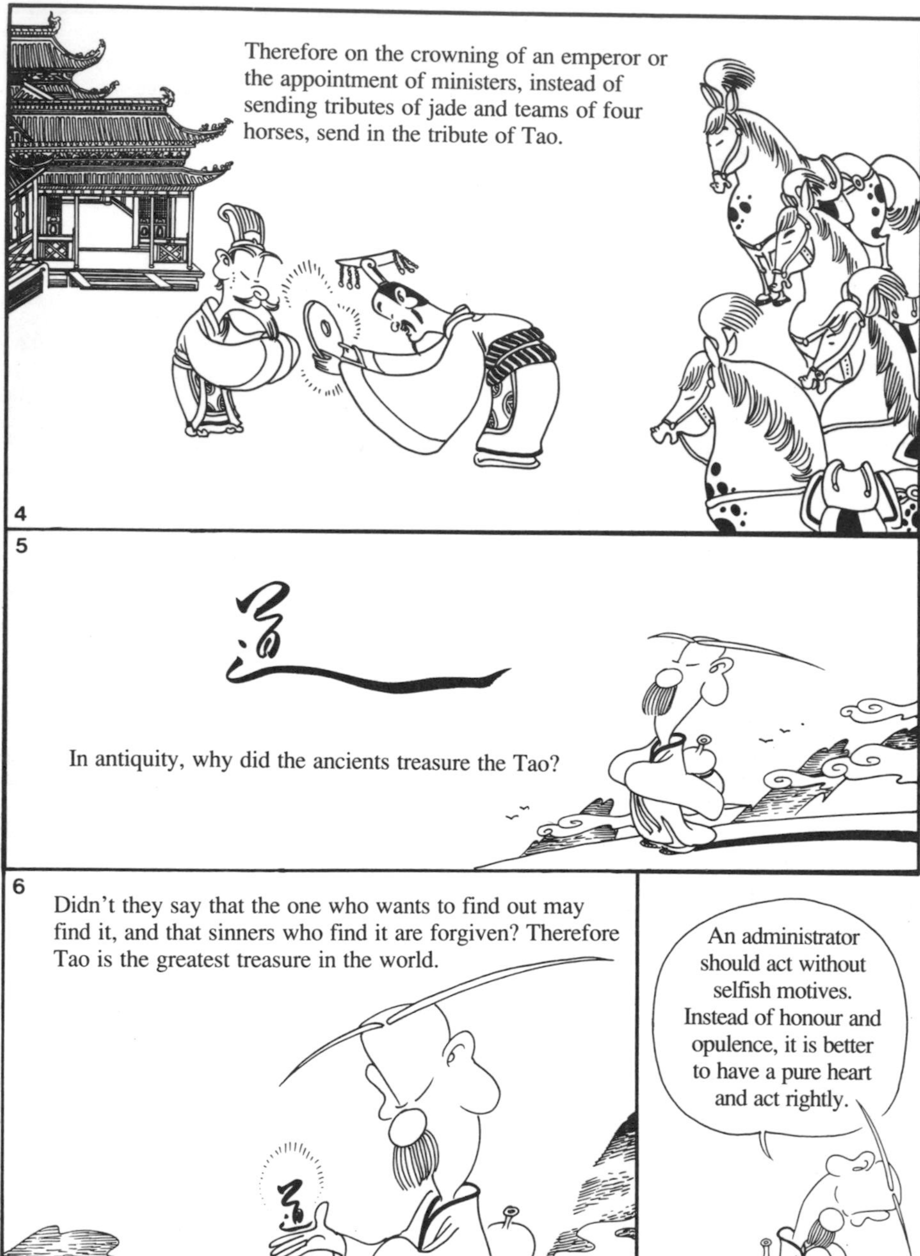
4
Therefore on the crowning of an emperor or the appointment of ministers, instead of sending tributes of jade and teams of four horses, send in the tribute of Tao.
5
In antiquity, why did the ancients treasure the Tao?
6
Didn't they say that the one who wants to find out may find it, and that sinners who find it are forgiven? Therefore Tao is the greatest treasure in the world.
An administrator should act without selfish motives. Instead of honour and opulence, it is better to have a pure heart and act rightly.

Difficult and easy

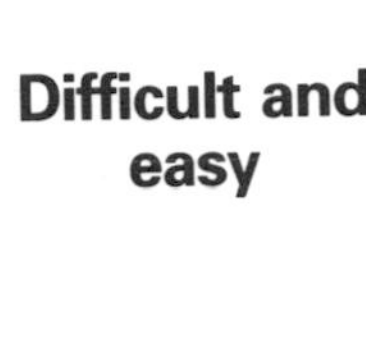

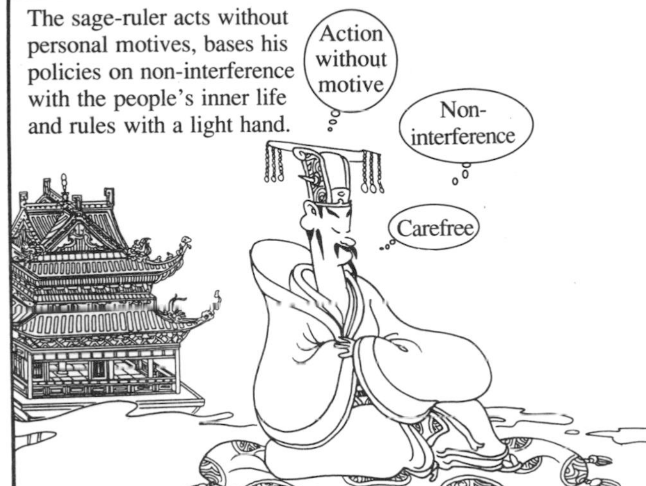

The sage-ruler acts without personal motives, bases his policies on non-interference with the people's inner life and rules with a light hand.
Action without motive
Non-interference
Carefree
1

Take difficult tasks in hand while they are easy.
2

And great affairs too while they are small.
3

The difficult problems of the world must be dealt with while they are yet easy. The great problems of the world must be dealt with while they are yet small.
4

5
The sage, then, throughout his life does nothing great and yet achieves a greatness of his own.
I will accomplish this tough task without fail!
He who lightly makes promises will surely be found wanting in good faith.
6
He who often underestimates difficult tasks will surely be beset with difficulties.
Light
Heavy
7
Because the sage is always aware of the existence of difficulties and never treats things lightly, he never encounters difficulties.
Difficult
Easy
8
When dealing with difficult things, tackle them while they are still manageable. When dealing with seemingly easy things, do not be too casual but undertake the task wholeheartedly so as not to risk failure.

Beginning and end

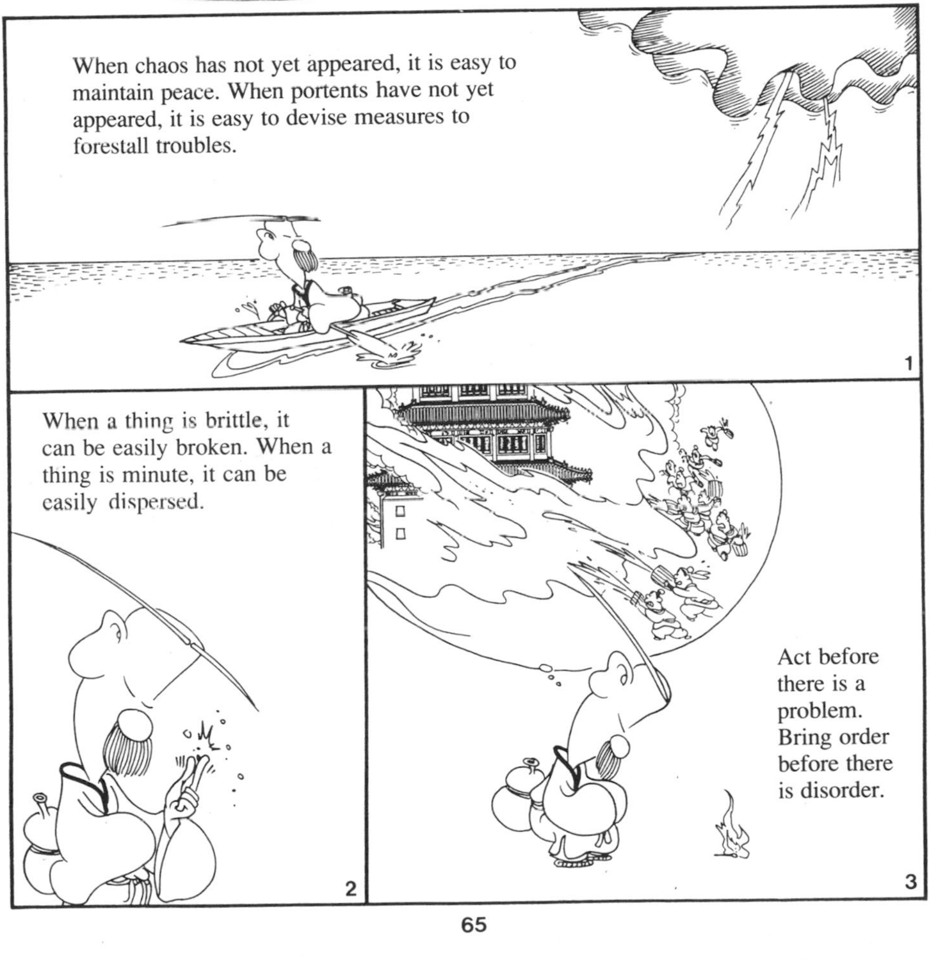

When chaos has not yet appeared, it is easy to maintain peace. When portents have not yet appeared, it is easy to devise measures to forestall troubles.

1

When a thing is brittle, it can be easily broken. When a thing is minute, it can be easily dispersed.

2

Act before there is a problem. Bring order before there is disorder.

3

* One li is about a third of a mile or a kilometre.

Wisdom and not knowledge

1

The rulers of old who were adept in the Tao did not make the people pursue knowledge, but kept them in the state of simplicity.

2

How am I to subjugate the people?

The people are difficult to govern when they are full of wiles.

How are we to thwart the government?

3

Therefore the ruler who relies on human-conceived knowledge does harm to the state. The ruler who does not rely on such knowledge does good to the state.

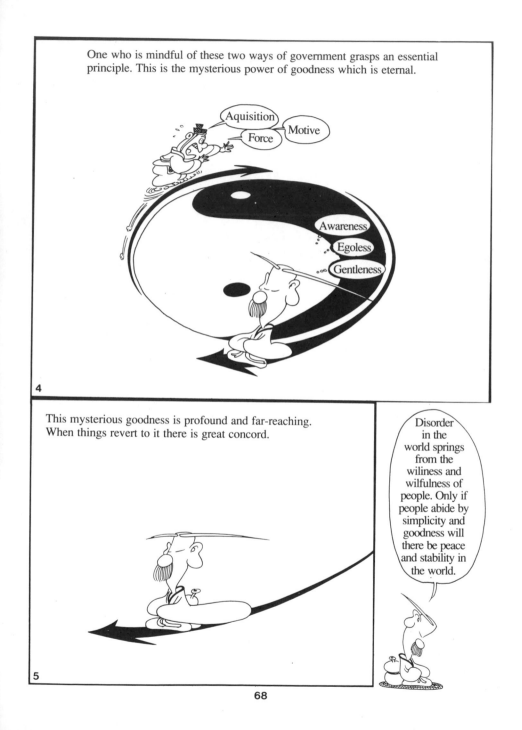

One who is mindful of these two ways of government grasps an essential principle. This is the mysterious power of goodness which is eternal.

4

This mysterious goodness is profound and far-reaching. When things revert to it there is great concord.

5

The three treasures

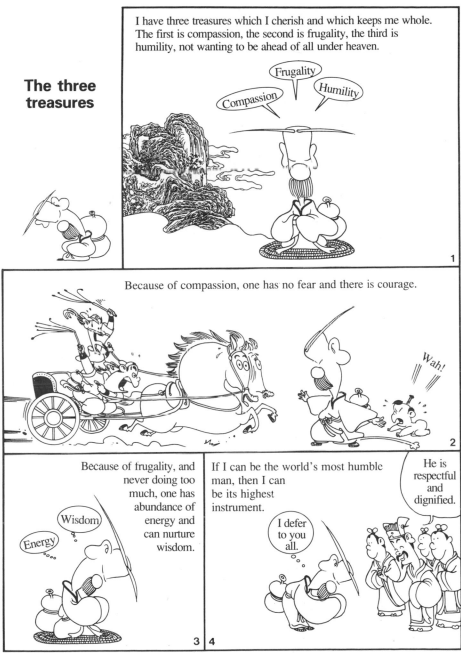

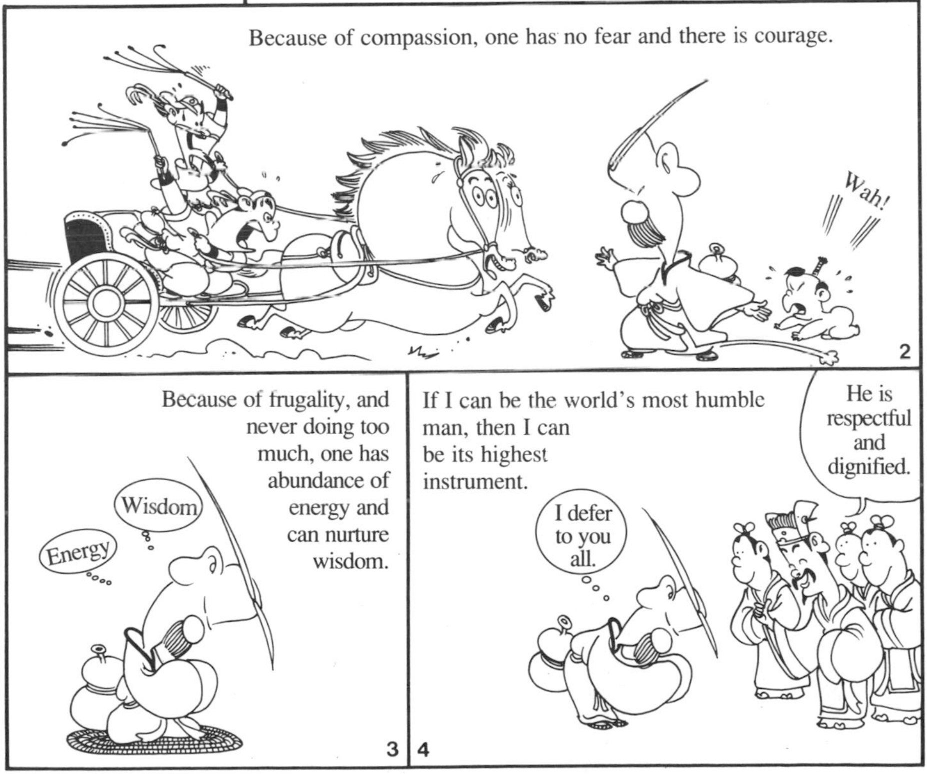

I have three treasures which I cherish and which keeps me whole. The first is compassion, the second is frugality, the third is humility, not wanting to be ahead of all under heaven.

1

Because of compassion, one has no fear and there is courage.

2

Because of frugality, and never doing too much, one has abundance of energy and can nurture wisdom.

3

If I can be the world's most humble man, then I can be its highest instrument.

4

5
If one forsakes love and seeks to be daring...
6
Forsakes restraint and seeks to be eminent...
7
Forsakes following behind and rushes in front, then he is doomed!
I won't give way!
8
Of the three treasures, compassion is the most important. When there is compassion, one can overcome all in an offensive war and repel all in a defensive war.
9
Because of the compassion of such a man, heaven will shelter and protect him.
Love and compassion form the basis of human relationship. If people can be like nature which nurtures all impartially, then the world will be free of strife.

The value of non-contention

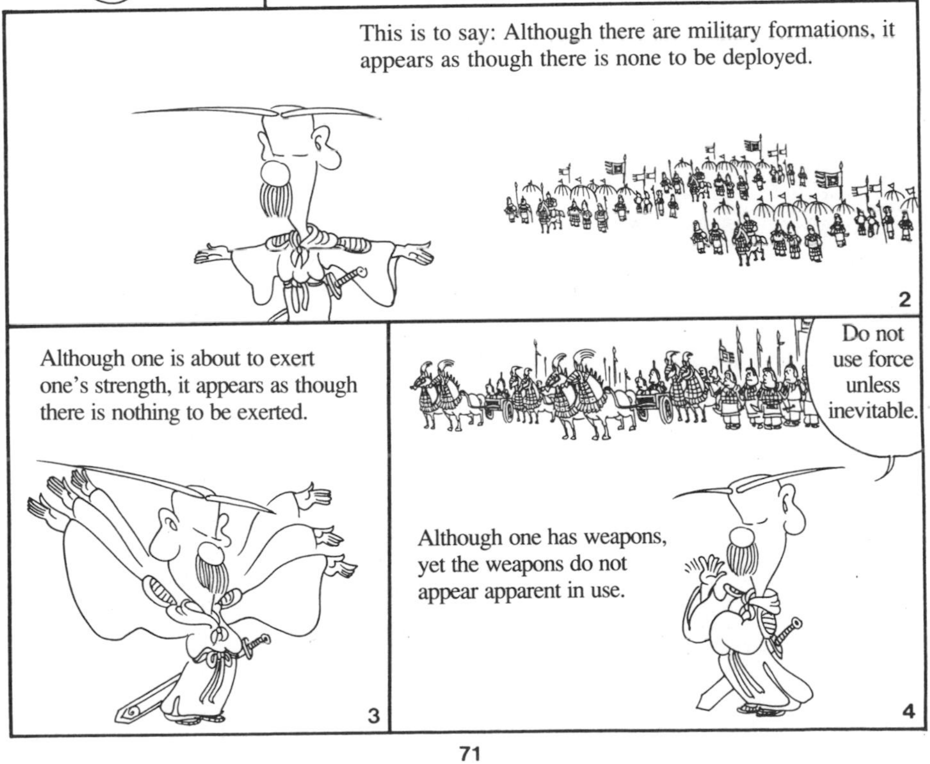

This is to say: Although there are military formations, it appears as though there is none to be deployed.

2

Although one is about to exert one's strength, it appears as though there is nothing to be exerted.

3

Do not use force unless inevitable.

Although one has weapons, yet the weapons do not appear apparent in use.

4

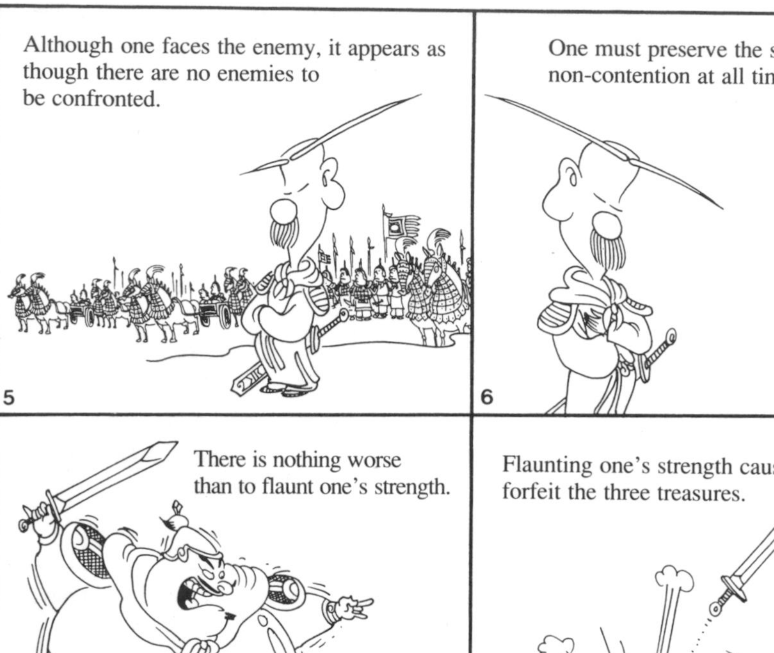

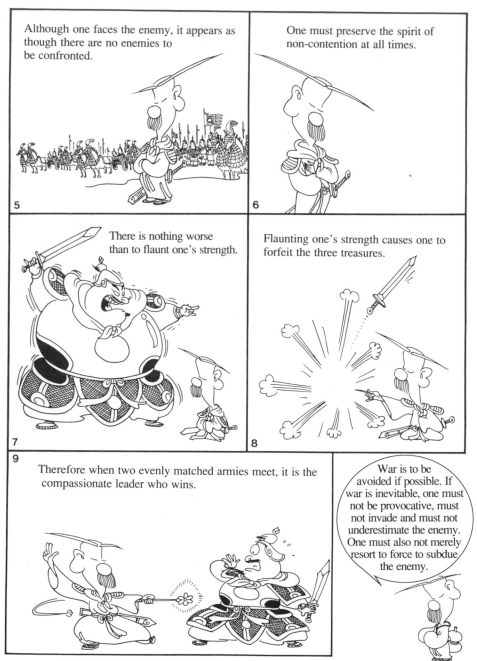

5
Although one faces the enemy, it appears as though there are no enemies to be confronted.
6
One must preserve the spirit of non-contention at all times.
7
There is nothing worse than to flaunt one's strength.
8
Flaunting one's strength causes one to forfeit the three treasures.

9
Therefore when two evenly matched armies meet, it is the compassionate leader who wins.

War is to be avoided if possible. If war is inevitable, one must not be provocative, must not invade and must not underestimate the enemy. One must also not merely resort to force to subdue the enemy.

Unknown sage

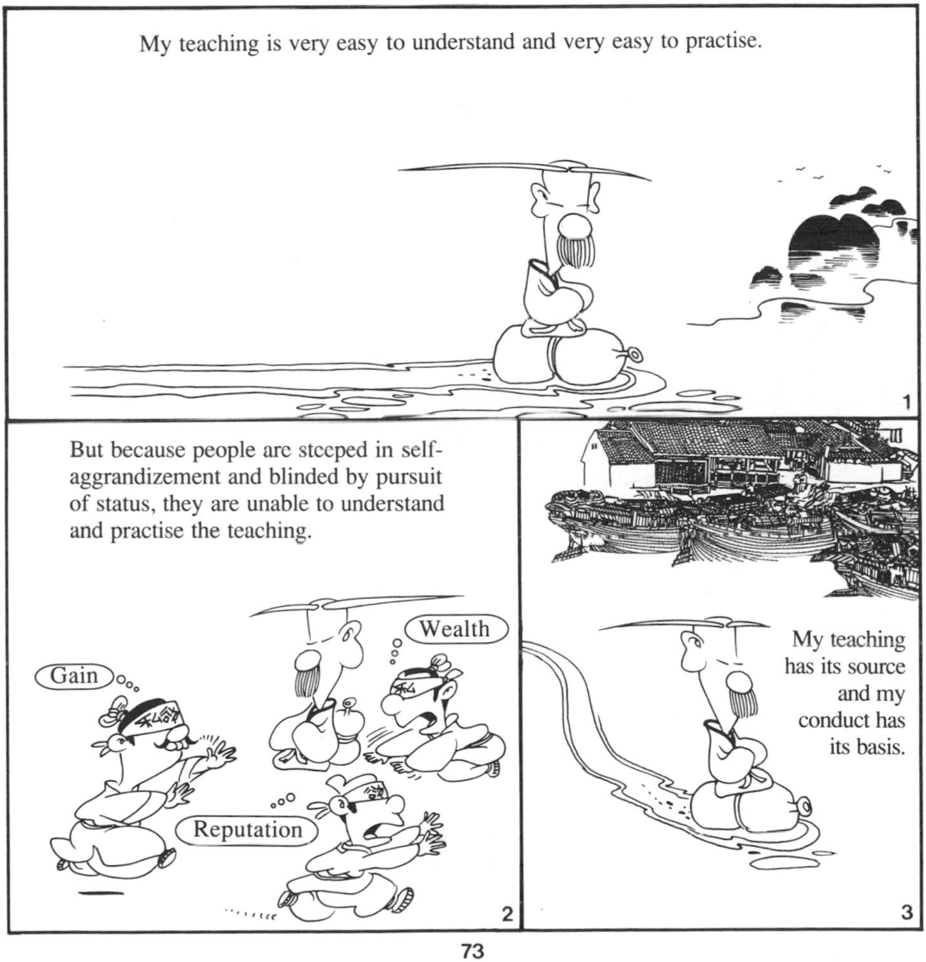

My teaching is very easy to understand and very easy to practise.

1

But because people are steeped in self-aggrandizement and blinded by pursuit of status, they are unable to understand and practise the teaching.

2

My teaching has its source and my conduct has its basis.

3

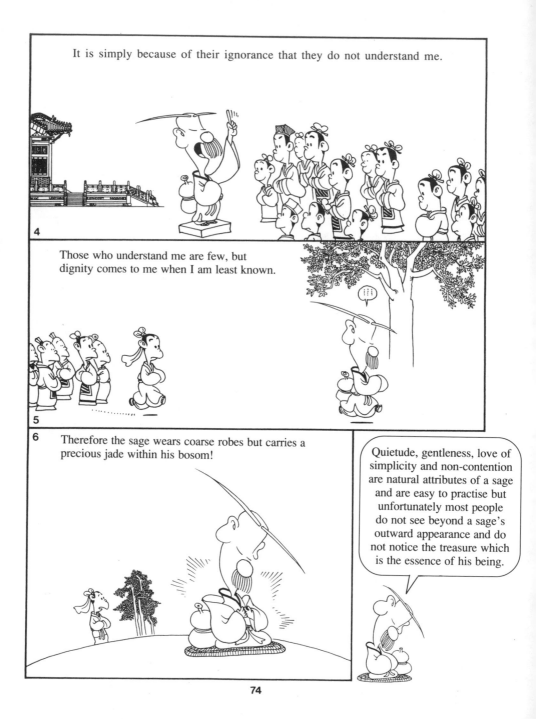

It is simply because of their ignorance that they do not understand me.
4
Those who understand me are few, but dignity comes to me when I am least known.
!!!!
5
6
Therefore the sage wears coarse robes but carries a precious jade within his bosom!
Quietude, gentleness, love of simplicity and non-contention are natural attributes of a sage and are easy to practise but unfortunately most people do not see beyond a sage's outward appearance and do not notice the treasure which is the essence of his being.

On punishment

When the people no longer fear the ruler's oppression and use of force...

1

2

...Then the exercise of authority will end in disaster.

Therefore the ruler must not oppress the people.

No more rice left.

Give!

3

The ruler must not cause the people to become weary of life.

4

5

Hence if the ruler does not oppress and ill treat the people, the people will not grow weary of him but will flock to him.

Therefore the sage knows himself and stands apart from others, but he does not make a show of it.

He has self-respect but does not feel self-important.

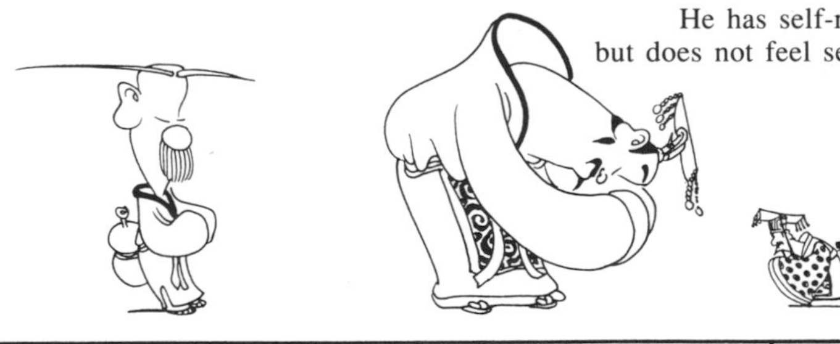

6

Therefore he abandons feelings of self-righteousness and self-importance and cherishes self-knowing and self-respect.

7

If a government is oppressive and deprives the people of their freedom and choice of livelihood, and when the people can no longer live in peace, they will rise in rebellion.

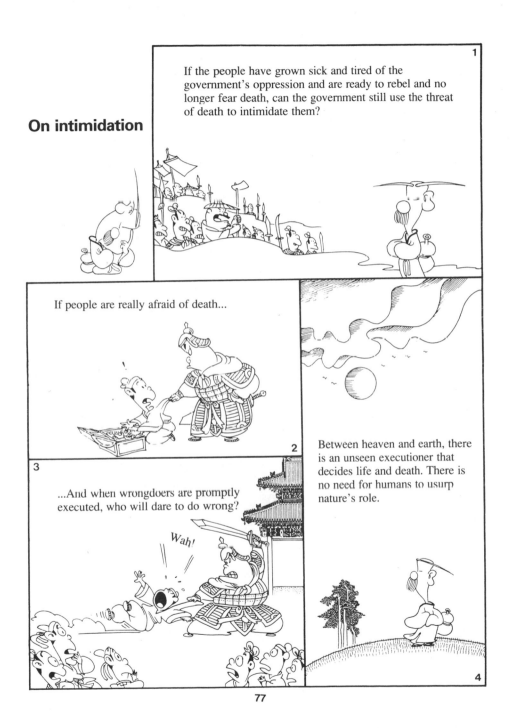

On intimidation

If the people have grown sick and tired of the government's oppression and are ready to rebel and no longer fear death, can the government still use the threat of death to intimidate them? 1

If people are really afraid of death...

2

3

...And when wrongdoers are promptly executed, who will dare to do wrong?

Between heaven and earth, there is an unseen executioner that decides life and death. There is no need for humans to usurp nature's role.

4

5
If humans try to usurp nature's role...
Let me mete out heavenly justice.
Let me chop it for you.
...Then it is like an unskilled man trying to do the work of a carpenter.
6
7
In so doing, the unskilled man seldom escapes injuring his own hands.
The natural world has its own law governing life and death. There is no need for a ruler to usurp nature's role and decide the fate of the people. He who tries to usurp nature's role cannot avoid bringing injury to himself.

No fear of death

The people suffer hunger because the ruler levy too many taxes. That is why they starve.

More taxes and I will starve to death.

1

The people become difficult to govern because of too much interference by the rulers in their lives. That is why they are unruly.

One regulation after another, how to obey all of them?

2

3
The people do not fear death because the rulers interfere too much with their lives. That is why they risk death.
We can stand it no longer!
4
He who gives no thought to self-gratification and is pure and selfless is wiser than those who live for themselves.

To rule with severity and high-handedness is thc cause of disaster. When the people are pushed to the brink of starvation and death, they will inevitably stage a revolt.

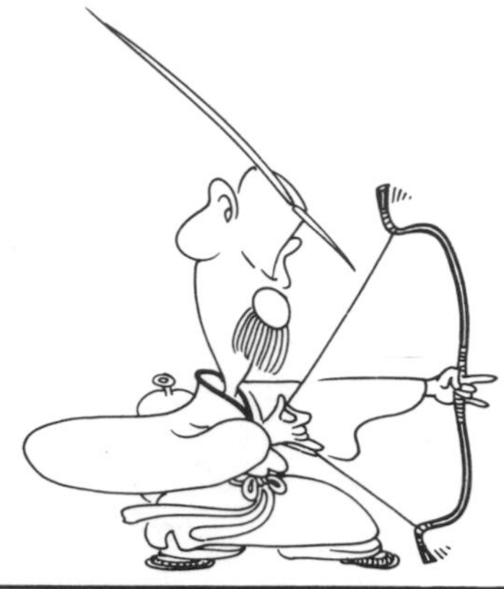

Bending the bow

Isn't the natural law like the bending of a bow?
1
The top comes down...
2
3
...And the bottom end goes up.
The extra length is shortened, the insufficient width is expanded.
4

The natural law is to reduce surplus and to make up for the scarcity
5
But the ways of men are to take away from those who do not have enough to give to those who have too much.
Robbing the poor to give to the rich!
For you!
Thank you!
6
Who can have an abundance to spare and to give it to the world?
7
Only the man of Tao can do so.
8
Nature's way is to diminish excess and replenish deficiency to ensure a balance. Society should abide by nature's way to ensure social harmony.

Utopia

1
The ideal state is:
The state should be
small and the inhabitants few.
Give me
a kati of
fruit.
2
Because of the absence of conflict,
there is no use for military devices.
3
There is no harsh and oppressive
ruler, so the people do not have to
risk their lives to migrate or travel
to distant places.
4
Though there are boats and
carriages, there is no need to
ride in them.
5
Though there are armour and
weapons, there is no need to
display them.
I have
wasted
fifty years
of my life
as a
soldier!

The ruler should make the people return to the state of pristine simplicity where the system of tying knots was used to keep records.
6
Then the people will be carefree and without desires. Though they have plain fare for food, they will consider it tasty and relish it.
7
Though the clothes they wear are patched, they consider themselves tastefully dressed.
8
Though they live in humble dwellings, they regard the houses as comfortable.
9
Though the customs are few and simple, the people enjoy them.
10

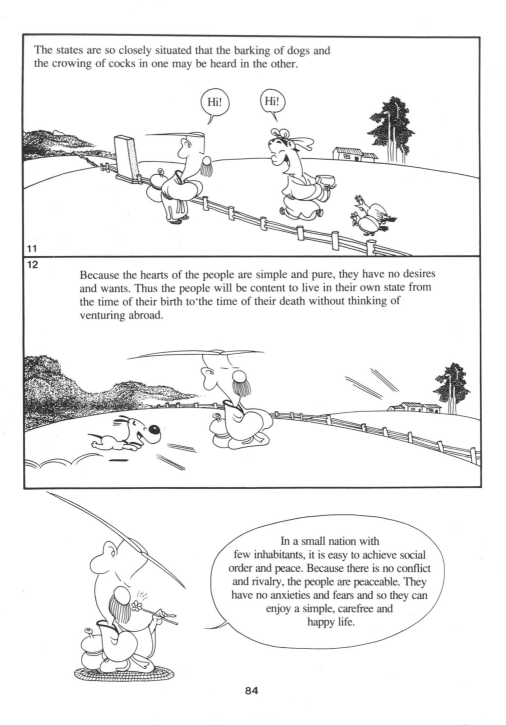

The states are so closely situated that the barking of dogs and the crowing of cocks in one may be heard in the other.

11

12

Because the hearts of the people are simple and pure, they have no desires and wants. Thus the people will be content to live in their own state from the time of their birth to the time of their death without thinking of venturing abroad.

In a small nation with few inhabitants, it is easy to achieve social order and peace. Because there is no conflict and rivalry, the people are peaceable. They have no anxieties and fears and so they can enjoy a simple, carefree and happy life.

《亚太漫画系列》

智者的低语

老子说II

编著：蔡志忠
翻译：许国强

亚太图书(新)有限公司出版

Coming soon...

A new and unique look
for these popular Chinese classics.
Edited and illustrated by
Tsai Chih Chung.

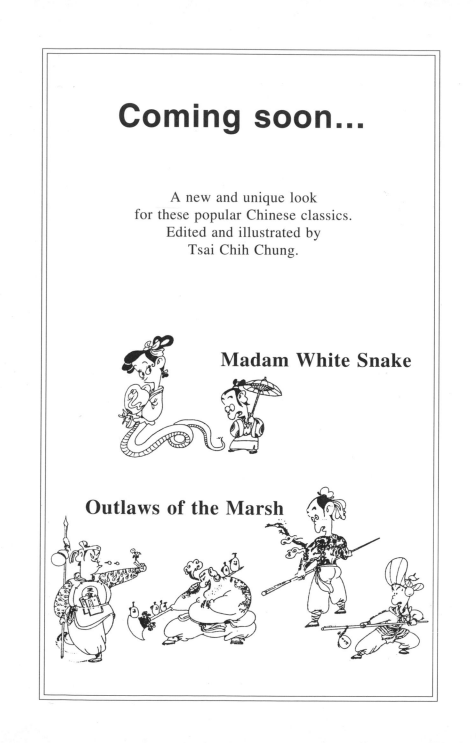

Madam White Snake

Outlaws of the Marsh